Half for You and Half for Me

Written by Shelly Hurst Lonni & Illustrated by Patrick Campbell

1 red apple in my hand,
but none for Mary Lou.

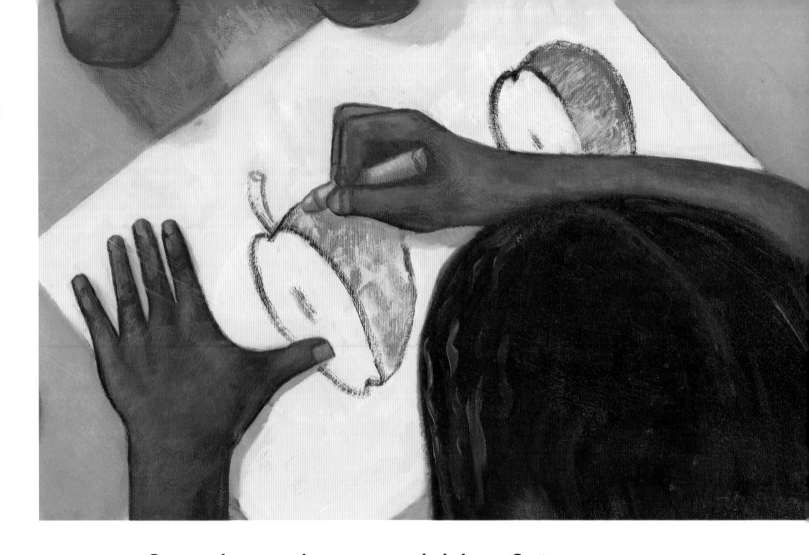

2 red apples would be fair.
Let's think what we should do.

If Mom cuts it into halves,
that's how we will get 2.

Half for you and half for me.
It is what best friends do.

1 big maple bar I have,
but none for Joe or Dee.

Since sharing is important,
I'll split it into 3.

A piece for Joe, a piece for Dee,
and a piece just for me!

1 pizza pie is all I have.
3 friends are at my door.

If Mom cuts it up 4 ways,
I'll have enough for 4.

A great big piece for Tai, and me,
and Tansy, and Lenore.

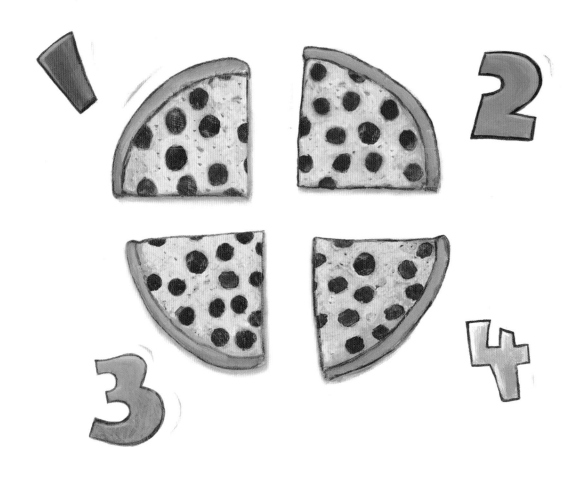

Mom cut the pizza equally,
but I wish we had more!